D1153369

B100 000003 2124 44

Hilke's Diary

Germany, July 1940–August 1945

In Honour of Hilke

I dedicate this book to my ten grandchildren, Phoebe, Lara, Thomas, Catherine, Jonathan, Francis, Rebecca, Isabelle, Alex and Lewis, and to all young people across the world.

Hilke's Diary

Germany, July 1940–August 1945

Edited by Geseke Clark

TEMPUS

First published 2008

Tempus Publishing
Cirencester Road, Chalford,
Stroud, Gloucestershire, GL6 8PE
www.thehistorypress.co.uk

Tempus Publishing is an imprint of The History Press

British Library Cataloguing in Publication Data.
A catalogue record for this book is available from the British Library.

ISBN 978 0 7524 4513 7

Typesetting and origination by The History Press
Printed in Great Britain by Ashford Colour Press Ltd, Gosport, Hampshire

Contents

Acknowledgements

It is with deep respect and affection that I present the wartime diary of my sister, Hilke. This is the personal story of a young girl growing up in Germany during the Second World War – away from home, with all the pain of homesickness and the challenge of daily life in a strange family – becoming a drama of survival and finally triumph. It is also the account of a young teenager who yearns to be a patriot, but whose heart cannot be reconciled with the suffering and injustice brought about by the war.

I would like to acknowledge with thanks the encouragement and help of my friend Elizabeth Ryder and my family in England, Germany and the United States.

Information about the *Deutsche Heimschule* comes courtesy of Scwester Teresia-Benedicta Kanzler from the Monastery Hegne.

Thanks go to Pascal Caudebec from Kall Kwik, Leamington Spa, for designing the maps.

Foreword

Hilke's diary is a battered, chintz-covered little book. The colours of the flowery pattern have faded over the nearly seventy years of its life and the open brass lock has lost its key. Its mere existence is remarkable as it survived being carried in a tightly packed rucksack on the back of a sixteen-year-old girl as she trekked for several dangerous and uncertain months across post-war Germany from the far south back to Hamburg in the north where she used to live.

Would the house she had grown up in still be there? Would her parents, her brother and sisters still be alive? There were no trains and there was no postal or telephone service. Germany was divided into four zones, the French, American, British and Russian. At each border one was required to have a pass which this girl did not have and was not able to obtain as she had no official residence.

This girl was my older sister, Hilke, who started the diary in 1940 when she was twelve, in the middle of the Second World War. It reveals a remarkable story of courage, honesty and self-reliance, and also of carrying responsibilities beyond her young age.

The diary is written in German in the old Gothic script. About a year ago I felt that since there were not many people alive able to read the old Gothic script and, furthermore, as my four children and ten grandchildren live in England, I had to transcribe and then translate it into English, so that one day they could read it.

I lent the manuscript to a brother-in-law and a nephew and their reaction prompted me to go further and make the story available not only to my family but to other readers, particularly to young people whose great-grandfathers might have fought the great-grandfather of my grandchildren.

I hope this story will, in a small way, help young readers of today to deepen their understanding of the effects of war on other children and on a nation like theirs. Could it also inspire them to see that basically we are all one big human family? No matter to which country we belong, across the border are brothers and sisters with similar problems and joys to our own. I hope this moving story might motivate some of our young people to work towards making this world a better, more peaceful place.

Our father, Curt, in First World War uniform (right), with his brother Rudolph.

Our father in his early forties.

Father playing tennis.

I want to say a little about our parents. Our father was a well-respected lawyer in Hamburg. He had a good sense of humour and a love of sport. He was an excellent tennis player who in 1933, for example, represented Germany in a tournament in Brighton. During the Hitler-period there was a certain amount of fear because he had a Jewish grandmother. It was not foreseeable whether this would be reason enough to be deported. In the end he was not deported, because he was careful. However, towards the end of the war he was not allowed to practise as a lawyer and had to work in a shipping yard. As he suffered badly from asthma he did not have to join the army. Like most of their friends, our parents did not know about the extent of cruelty during the years of the Holocaust.

Our mother, Lottie, in her early thirties (left) *and with her first two children, Henning and Hilke,* c.1932 (right).

Our mother was a strong, courageous and cultured woman interested in matters of the spirit. She was brought up with Victorian values which later she questioned profoundly. Like all mothers she loved her children deeply, yet her love was not possessive, not sentimental. This, together with her great trust in God, made it possible for her to let her children be evacuated so far away from home. She must have worried and yearned for them, but her main concern was for their safety. In Germany the evacuation of children was not organised by the government as it was in England. Each family had to arrange this privately and finding a suitable family was not easy. We children were often desperately homesick. Sometimes we did not see our parents for six months or more. Once, after I had written that I was not getting on with the girl for whom I was meant to be a companion, I received a long and strict letter from my mother saying that I had to remember that I was a guest in the family and should not quarrel with any of the children.

My sister wrote this diary of her own accord, without help or prompting from anybody. I do not think that our mother or anybody else was ever invited to read it. Within its pages people and events from the Hitler-era are seen through her young eyes. Her comments and views are her own, and possibly those of her school teachers, but not of our parents, for whom it was, alas, dangerous to express an honest opinion in front of their children.

Geseke Clark
Warwick, England, 2007

Hilke as a young child,
c.1932.

Hilke, c.1935.

Hilke's Diary

D. 21. 7. 1940.

Dieses Tagebuch wollte ich als ich gerade 4 Monate von Hamburg u. meinen Eltern getrennt war. Ich fuhr am 21.12.1939 nach Wuischkeim zu Onkel Harald u. Tante Grete. Es war ein sehr kalter Winter. Ich ging oft wandern u. in den Wald, um Rehe u. Hasen zu sehen.

Diesem Tagebuch will ich nun mein Freud u. Leid anvertrauen.

————

The first page of Hilke's diary.

27th July 1940

I was given this diary when I had been separated from Hamburg and my parents for exactly seven months. On 27th December I arrived here in Meisenheim to stay with Uncle Herbert and Aunt Erika. It was a very cold winter. I often went tobogganing and walking in the wood and saw deer and hares.

To this diary I will entrust both my joys and sorrows.

4th August 1940

Today I received a letter which said that my parents want me to stay here until 1st September. The holidays have been extended.

5th August 1940

Today I saw a swarm of bees fly out. They were hanging like a bunch of grapes on the tree. Then the beekeeper came and collected them from the tree. I went quite close to it.

A sample of a honeycomb.

16th August 1940

We were on a visit to Hamburg. During the night of 14th to 15th there was an air raid. We had to go into the cellar for two hours. My first serious air raid!

Den 2.7.1941. Am 22.6. ist Krieg mit Rußland ausgebrochen.

Die englischen Fliegerangriffe waren im Mai besonders schlimm. 3 Nächte werde ich nie vergessen. Dicht bei der Hamburg... fielen... Bomben, die ein ... schmauß... In der ...gang sind ganze Straßen eingestürzt. Der ...fen brannte bis Morgens 11 Uhr. Die Post war ...düst, der Ring hatte ein ...werk eingebüßt, ...

Summer 1940 in Meisenheim.

23rd August 1940

Today I went with Uncle Herbert and Aunt Erika to the deer park. The deer and roebucks, including a pure white one, were eating out of my hand.

28th August 1940

Today I have been away from home exactly eight months and one day. I am missing Mummy and Daddy desperately.

8th September 1940

Mummy and Daddy visited us in Meisenheim. After eight months and twelve days I saw my parents again. I went to meet them at Bad Kreuznach, so that I could be alone with them for two hours. I told them everything: about Uncle Herbert's outbursts of rage and Aunt Erika's bad moods. Also, that they were short of money. Sadly, after two days, Mummy and Daddy left again for Hamburg.

Left: *Hilke, c.1934.*

Below: *Hilke in a tracksuit, c.1937.*

27th September 1940

Today I have been away from Hamburg for exactly three quarters of a year. Today we have been filmed as a Christmas present for Mummy and Daddy. Tomorrow Henning will go back to Hamburg, because school starts again on September 30th. We three girls (Geseke, Brigitte and me) will stay here.

Geseke by the river Alster in Hamburg, 1938.

Far left: *Brigitte before the war.*

Left: *Henning, Hilke and Geseke, c.1937.*

4th November 1940

Today a letter arrived from Mummy, in which she announced her first great victory over Daddy in table tennis. I was glad about that, and Mummy is so proud.

29th December 1940

Today I have been away from Hamburg for a year and two days. I was meant to go home for Christmas, but a middle ear inflammation has prevented this plan. As Uncle Herbert is ill, Aunt Erika is very busy and we are not often allowed to go into the Christmas room. So I am very aware that Christmas at home with my parents is much more lovely than here.

20th January 1941

After Aunt Erika had again been in a bad mood I wrote a letter to Henning to say that Aunt Erika has too much to do and that she would like us to return to Hamburg. As a result Mummy wrote that Daddy would come to collect us in February. I am so looking forward to being back in Hamburg.

Three days ago, while I was tobogganing with the school, I fell on the ice. I got an open wound at the back of my head and had to see the doctor. Today Henning wrote that Mummy was ill again. She has given notice to our cook Trude.

21st March 1941

On 18th February 1941 I arrived back in Hamburg. At last, after a year and a half, back home again! I am very happy at home. I am back at school where a lot has changed. I have to catch up a lot. Often Henning can go to the cinema while I have to do sums. That is hard on me! Henning gives Mummy a lot of trouble nowadays, because he is always contradicting her. Air raids are not so bad at the moment.

Geseke playing a mouth organ, c.1940.

2nd and 9th June 1941

Edel sei der Mensch, hilfreich und gut. (Goethe)
Noble be ye, helpful and good.

Denn je grösser der Mensch, desto verträglicher ist er im Zorn, und ein edles Gemüt fühlt sich zur Güte geneigt. (Ovid)
The greater a man, the more conciliatory he is in his anger, and a noble mind is inclined to do good.

Quotations by Goethe and Ovid, and photograph of Odenbach.

2nd July 1941

On June 22nd the war with Russia began. The English air raids in May were pretty bad. Three nights I shall never forget. Near the Lombards Bridge a bomb fell and destroyed a signalman's hut.

In the harbour area whole streets have collapsed. The harbour was on fire until 11 o'clock in the morning. The main post office was damaged and the big insurance building known as the 'Ring' has lost a floor. Neither the suburban trains nor the trams are working. In short, the whole city was in chaos.

Because of the bombing raids our nanny, Fräulein Paula, Henning and I had gone to the Lüneburger Heath. I liked it there. We lived in a farm house with a thatched roof and no electric light. It was also a sort of inn. The 'Totengrund' I shall not forget so easily. We found three young hares there. The mother was gone and a hawk was circling over the nest. We took the three young hares home. One died on the way, and I put it under a fir tree. The two others we took back to Hamburg. As they could not drink by themselves, we had to take a straw and pour milk down their throats. After three weeks the second one died. The third one we called Heidi. Now Heidi is big enough to drink on her own. It is so funny when she cleans herself.

3rd July 1941

I have been selected to take part in the swimming races of the Jungmädel [Hitler Youth Group for Girls]. I am the second best in our region and have to join the Obergau Wettschwimmen [inter-county swimming competition], of which I am very proud.

Hilke's description of her teachers at her school in Meisenheim, 1941. The translation runs:

1. 20 lines! You pigs! You deserve a good hiding!
2. Ah! My old friend. She is playing with her key.
3. What do you think you are doing? Write ten times, 'I must sharpen my pencil properly'.
4. You must be completely mad! Ten pages of lines.

These are the characters, sentences and peculiarities of my four teachers in Meisenheim. Their names are: 1) Mr Wiemann 2) Miss Baumanns 3) Mr Engels 4) Mr Nell

17th July 1941

Finally the holidays have arrived. My report is as follows:

Arithmetic 4; Geography 4; Gym-apparatus-work: 4 (about which I am v. disappointed); English 4; Drawing 4; German 3; Biology 3; Singing 3 (which surprises me); Gymnastic 3; Handwriting 3; History 3.★

Tomorrow we are going into the Harz Mountains; I am really looking forward to it. At last, my wish to see these mountains is fulfilled. I am especially looking forward to the fir trees. We are going to Hahnenklee. I hope we will find many blueberries. I hope the clover will bring me good luck on our trip to the Harz and Altgarge.

28th September 1941

It was lovely in Hahnenklee, although it rained almost all the time. We found many mushrooms which we took back to Hamburg and bottled. Such dark fir trees! Lovely!

The other day we had another air raid. Henning and I were alone with the live-in home help, as Mummy and Daddy had gone to Meisenheim to fetch Geseke and Brigitte. There were seventy-four dead. In my school, too, there was an incident. In the playground and in front of the school are unexploded bombs which have laid there for several days. They are so dangerous because they could explode any moment. All the windows are broken. Luckily the Heilwig School has one main building and one annexe. Now we

---

★ *1 is the best mark and very rare, 6 is the worst and also very rare.*

have to go into the main building every afternoon from 2 p.m. until 6 p.m. That is not nice, because I cannot go on the outings to the Elbe on Saturdays with the rest of the family.

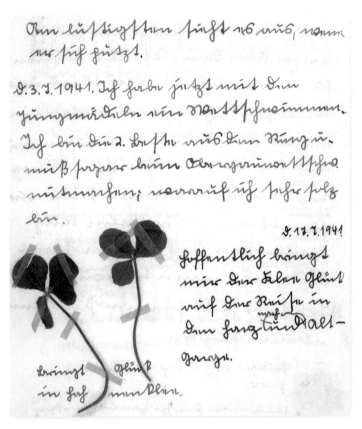

Hilke hoped that the clover would bring her good luck for the trip into the Harz Mountains.

Left: *Geseke with our father in 'Planten un Blomen', a park in Hamburg.*
Right: *Hilke with Brigitte, 1941.*

The other day they all went to Hagenbeck's Zoo, but I was on duty with the Hitler Youth Group.

Geseke, now 7½ years of age, and Brigitte, 4 years, have come home again. Brigitte has grown. She still looks like me. I like her better than Geseke who is often silly and acts like a monkey. She doesn't exactly obey either. But I don't have quarrels with her. Aunt Erika and Uncle Herbert are going to move to Rheydt, as Uncle H. has been promoted. I am now learning Spanish as a second foreign language.

Newspaper Cutting of 11th October 1941

Announcement of the Supreme Command of the Armed Forces

The battle on the Sea of Azov has ended. In collaboration with the air-fleet of Air Chief Marshal Löhr, the army of General von Manstein's infantry has defeated the Romanian army of General Dumitrescu. The tank-unit of

Chief-Marshal von Kleist has routed the greater part of the 9th and 18th Soviet army. After heavy loss of life 64,325 prisoners, 126 tanks, 519 heavy artillery and countless other war material have been seized. Together with the above mentioned armies and the allied Italian, Hungarian and Slovakian troops the army of Field Marshal von Rundstedt has since September 26th taken 106,356 prisoners as well as 212 tanks and 672 heavy artillery.

Newspaper Cutting of 16th October 1941, Bucharest

The Supreme Command of the Romanian army made the following announcement on Thursday:

Our troops have broken through the defence line by Odessa. The enemy is retreating along the whole of the front… The advance continues. Odessa is in flames.

3rd November 1941

First snow.

19th November 1941

Air raid from 9–11.30. Two bombs hit the main station, one on platform 2 and one by the luggage counter.

Today we learnt at school about coping with incendiary bombs. On Thursday we are going from school to a demonstration to show us how. I wonder whether we will have to practise extinguishing such a bomb by ourselves.

Zwei sowjetische Armeen vernichtet

Aus dem Führerhauptquartier, 11. Oktober

Das Oberkommando der Wehrmacht gil bekannt:

Die Schlacht am Asowschen Meer ist abgeschlossen. Im Zusammenwirken mit der Luftflotte des Generalobersten Loehr hai die Armee des Generals der Infanterie von Manstein, die rumänische Armee des Korpsgenerals Dumitrescu und die Panzerarmee des Generalobersten von Kleist die Masse der 9. und 18. sowjetischen Armee geschlagen und vernichtet. Bei schweren blutigen Verlusten hat der Gegner 64325 Gefangene, 126 Panzerkampfwagen, 519 Geschütze und unübersehbare Mengen an sonstigem Kriegsmaterial verloren.

Mit den genannten Armeen und den verbündeten italienischen, ungarischen und slowakischen Truppen hat die Heeresgruppe des Generalfeldmarschalls von Rundstedt seit dem 26. September nunmehr insgesamt 106365 Gefangene gemacht sowie 212 Panzerkampfwagen und 672 Geschütze erbeutet.

Einbruch in Odessa

dnb. Bukarest, 16. Oktober

Das Oberkommando der rumänischen Armee hat am Donnerstag folgende Meldung ausgegeben:

Unsere Truppen haben die Verteidigungslinie von Odessa durchbrochen. Der Feind befindet sich auf der ganzen Front im Rückzug. Guiliacovo, Dalnic und Tatarca sind seit acht Uhr in unserer Hand. Der Vormarsch geht weiter. Odessa brennt.

hauptſtadt der krim genommen

Aus dem Führerhauptquartier, 2. November

Das Oberkommando der Wehrmacht gibt bekannt:

In entſchloſſener Ausnützung unſeres Sieges auf der Krim wird die Verfolgung des geſchlagenen Gegners ſchwungvoll fortgeſetzt. Der Nordrand des Jaila-Gebirges iſt in breiter Front erreicht. Deutſche und rumäniſche Truppen haben geſtern Simferopol, die Hauptſtadt der Krim, genommen und befinden ſich in weiterem Vorgehen auf Sewaſtopol.

Newspaper Cutting of 2nd November 1941, from the Headquarters of the Führer

The Supreme Command of the Armed Forces announces:

The Capital of the Crimea taken. Building on the victory in the Crimea the beaten enemy is being vigorously pursued. The edges of the Jaila-Mountains have been reached along a wide front. German and Romanian troops have taken the capital of the Crimea, Simferopol, and are advancing on Sebastopol.

10th November 1941

At the moment I don't seem to get on with Geseke. When she was in Meisenheim I had been so looking forward to seeing her again. Instead she has become silly and naughty. She doesn't obey me at all and is only concerned with annoying me. Since Meisenheim I have tried many times to get on with her. For one day it works out very well, but then it is the same. Mummy always takes her side. She thinks we should go easy on her at the moment, but I think we cannot let her get away with everything. Our cook is annoyed that she gets woken up by the little ones at 6 o'clock and is about to give notice. Our nanny, Fräulein

Paula, is ill; therefore we cannot possibly do without the cook. Who knows how we will cope with Christmas, when chocolate, marzipan, coffee and much else will be free from rationing. Of course, we want to stock up for next year. On the other hand, Christmas should be lovely and the tree doesn't get into the room beautifully decorated all by itself. These are all difficulties that one doesn't worry about in times of peace.

Newspaper Cutting

Offensive target: Civilian Homes.

The main focus of the British air raids in Hamburg on the night of 16th September was aimed, as so often, at civilian homes.

Angriffsziel: Wohnviertel

Der Schwerpunkt des britischen Luftangriffs auf Hamburg in der Nacht zum 16. September richtete sich, wie schon so oft, wieder gegen Wohnviertel

30th November 1941

Today is the first day of Advent. It was difficult to get an Advent tree. All the wreaths had been sold out for five days. You couldn't even get fir tree branches.

Aunt Elise [Nottebohm] has invited us in spite of the war. For the fiftieth time Father Christmas is going to be there. Henning is already too old for that, that's why he won't come this time. It will also be the last time for me.

In November 1941 our great hero Werner Mölders was killed. There was a ceremony for him in Berlin. Mummy said that all heroes have to die some time. Günter Prien also died the death of a hero.

Mölders had shot down 116 aeroplanes. He was the greatest air force hero Germany has ever had. 'A nation which has heroes like that is destined for victory', that's what Field Marshal Goering said at Mölders' graveside.

Cotton grass (found on the heath). Cotton grass is a bog plant. That's why I found it in a little muddy pond…

17th December 1941

There was a bad air raid in the night of December 1st. Two explosive bombs fell quite near to us. Eight people died in one house. Friends of mine were among the dead. Eight houses were so badly damaged that they had to be blown up. Two cranes are clearing away the rubble. The place has been on fire for three days. All in all, this one air raid killed sixty-one people.

19th December 1941

Yesterday we had our reports:

Gymnastics 3; German 3; History 3; Art 3; Needlework 4; Singing 3; Mathematics 4; English 5; Spanish 3; Handwriting 2.

At last the holidays have arrived; no more school for eighteen days!

Cotton grass found on the heath.

31st December 1941

Today is 31st December 1941. May the year 1942 bring us peace. This is the last time that I shall write 1941.

9th April 1942

Today Mummy told me that she is expecting her fifth child at the end of September. At first I was speechless, but now I am really looking forward to it. At the end of May I will be going to Hungary with the HJ [Hitler Youth Group]. I am looking forward to it. It will be my first trip abroad.

30th July 1942

The trip to Hungary didn't happen. Since 15th June I have instead been on an estate near Würzburg to be educated together with the daughter there. The newspaper advertisement said: 'We are looking for a thirteen-year-old girl as a school friend for our daughter, class 3, Grammar School, wooded area, estate near Würzburg'

The estate is 400 acres. Asta, my comrade, is blond with blue eyes and delicate. She has a dog and twenty-five rabbits. The estate has four more dogs, fifteen cows, one bull, three hundred sheep and twelve horses with many foals. I can go horse riding and have made good progress. Asta and I have a private teacher at the house. After the holidays I shall have French. Asta doesn't do Spanish. In Hamburg I would have to repeat the course again. I don't know what will happen later.

7th August 1942

During these holidays I am staying with Aunt Erika again in Rheydt. I saw Geseke and Brigitte again. We have a lot of air raids. On Sunday we had to go to the bunker. The first time in a public air-raid shelter! In the evening, when we were in a cinema, the alarm sounded. When we came home we heard a special news bulletin: a town in the Caucasian mountains had been taken at 6.20 p.m. and by 8.45 p.m. everyone in Germany heard about it.

Hilke (far right) during her evacuation on the estate Waldschwind near Würzburg, 1943. She writes, 'We all helped to put up the sheaves of oats. The baron took the photo.'

Sample of the grey, paper-like material that a wasp produces when building a nest, and the twig of a date tree.

Pass allowing our family to get into the air-raid shelter.

Recently there were dreadful air raids in Hamburg and in Düsseldorf. Düsseldorf: 127 dead and 189,000 homeless. Aunt Erika has a brother there. She and I went to the – for me – unknown city. We went down the famous Königsallee which now looked very sad. No windows anywhere! Lots of broken roofs! Dirt, rubble, broken glass and damaged trees wherever we looked. Often whole districts with no roof undamaged. House after house destroyed. To think that people got out of there alive! Dr Göbbels spoke yesterday to the population of Düsseldorf. Many people are moving away.

Hamburg: 200–300 dead! Apart from Henning, luckily none of us were there. The letter from Mummy says:

Dear Children!
Now I am going to tell you about our dreadful air raid on 26th July 1942. It was a miracle that we have been spared, as was our neighbour Fischer's house on the right and the garage. (This house also belongs to us and Daddy wants to have both houses pulled down after the war and then sell the land.) But the Pohl's

house on the other side was burning, as well as the Gossler's house (two houses further on). Dr Hahn's house and the Dölles' house are completely burnt out (Geseke's friend lived there).

To the right of the garage incendiary bombs had fallen on the apartment block. Mummy's old school, too, at No.12, was on fire. Daddy and Henning have helped there, carrying files out etc. Then the house next to it, the milkman's house. Behind us, the students' kitchen and next to it, where Grütz lived. Everywhere there were enough helpers, partly because of the foreign workers. There was a fire, too. In fact, it was quite a spectacle! After the 'all-clear' the Hillers came round to look and they thought the whole street was on fire! They rang us at 3 p.m. to say they could take three of us for the night and were quite surprised that we didn't need to take up their offer.

The worst part was the hours at the beginning, as we were sitting in the air-raid shelter in the cellar listening to the whistling

The family's home in Hamburg (Klopstockstraße 29), demolished in 1965 to make room for the offices of an insurance company.

of the bombs. I looked to the right through the glass door onto the street and saw a sea of flames: six incendiary bombs in front of the house. I looked to my left through the glass door into the garden and again saw nothing but flames and thought, how do we get out, when our house will be on fire at any moment. But everything soon died down without setting our house alight.

Later, after the all-clear, the others stayed on the roof to make sure that the sparks flying through the streets would not set light to our house. From the roof the sight was eerily beautiful. All around us houses collapsed in flames: Neue Rabenstrasse and Fontenay, with its charming old houses, were destroyed. The Jungfernstieg, the famous shopping street in the centre of Hamburg, looks dreadful.

The Alsterpavillion, the well-known café, has gone, the Hamburger Hof is in ruins, the Dresdener Bank with its brand new top floor, is in ruins. The Neuer Wall is still on fire, as is the Hofbräu-Haus on the Stephans-Platz. Our household washing which was in Ohlsdorf at the laundry was burnt. Uhlenhorst, Barmbek, Eimsbüttel, Hammerbrook and St Georg are said to have been particularly badly hit. Daddy's secretary's house was hit by a bomb and she, at seventy years of age, is in a terrible state. And imagine, Daddy's partner, Dr Halben and his family in Mundsburg, have lost everything. They barely escaped with their lives.

Last night was not as bad. Our air defence started straight away with more support. The hospital in Eppendorf is apparently badly damaged because of a huge bomb.

1,000 greetings
Your Mummy

This was the second big air raid. The first was on 11th May 1941 (three nights) and the second on 26th July 1942. Was it God's hand that spared us? I thank Him, that He has protected my parents.

19th August 1942

Today, Aunt Erika, Uncle Herbert, Geseke and I went on a wonderful farewell trip, because I am leaving on Saturday. It was so lovely, who thinks of war! And today was such a meaningful day!

Newspaper Cuttings

A well-planned, large-scale landing of English, American, Canadian and De Gaulle troops, approximately the size of a division, arrived as a first wave on the mainland near Dieppe. It was under the protection of strong sea and air forces, led by tanks which had landed earlier. The entire attempt was defeated with heavy losses for the enemy. As of 4 p.m. today there is no further armed enemy presence on the mainland.

28 tanks which landed were later destroyed. All the strongholds have been held by our brave coastal forces. Over 1,500 prisoners are in German hands, among them 60 Canadian officers. Enemy losses are high. They have suffered a devastating defeat with this attempt to land, which while serving political purposes, stood no chance in reality. The German army guarding the coast has effortlessly repulsed this amateurish enterprise. It will meet any further attempts by the enemy with the calm and power of an army which has pinned victory to their flags in hundreds of battles.

20th August 1942

On 22nd August I will be going with Aunt Erika and her daughter, Ursula, to Meisenheim. There, Ursula will be left at a children's home and I will see Aunt Erika's dog Armin again.

Aus dem Führerhauptquartier, 19. August. Das Oberkommando der Wehrmacht gibt bekannt:

Eine groß angelegte Landung englischer, amerikanischer, kanadischer und de=Gaulle= Truppen in der Stärke etwa einer Division als erste Welle, die in den heutigen Morgenstunden gegen die französische Kanalküste bei Dieppe unter dem Schutz starker See= und Luftstreit= kräfte und unter Einsatz von gelandeten Pan= zern geführt wurde, ist durch die im Küsten= schutz eingesetzten deutschen Kräfte unter hohen blutigen Verlusten für den Gegner zusammengebrochen. Seit 16 Uhr befindet sich kein bewaffneter Feind mehr auf dem Festland.

Dazu kam es nicht. Der gelandete Feind wurde im Nahkampf überall aufgerieben und ins Meer geworfen. Von den gelandeten und später vernichteten Panzerkampfwagen sind bisher 28 gezählt. Alle Stützpunkte wurden von der tapferen Küsten= besatzung gehalten.

Über 1500 Gefangene befinden sich in deutscher Hand, darunter 60 kanadische Offiziere. Die blutigen Verluste des Feindes sind sehr hoch.

Durch Artilleriefeuer wurden drei Zer= störer, zwei Torpedoboote und zwei Transporter versenkt. Die Luftwaffe schoß 83 feindliche Flugzeuge ab, versenkte zwei Spezial=Truppentransportern und ein Schnellboot und beschädigte fünf Kreu= zer oder große Zerstörer sowie zwei Trans= porter durch schwere Bombentreffer.

Der Feind hat bei diesem, nur politischen Zwecken dienenden, aber jeder militäri= schen Vernunft hohnsprechenden Lan= dungsversuch eine vernichtende Nie= derlage erlitten. Die deutsche Wacht im Westen hat dem dilettantenhaften Unternehmen die gebührende Abfuhr erteilt. Sie sieht im übrigen allen weiteren Versuchen dieses Geg= ners mit der Ruhe und Kraft einer Wehrmacht entgegen, die in Hunderten von Schlachten den Sieg an ihre Fahnen geheftet hat.

Heather collected on an outing with Aunt Erika, Uncle Herbert and Geseke before going back to Hamburg.

Then I will go back to the estate and Aunt Erika and Uncle Herbert will go on holiday. Lore, our 17-year-old nanny, will go with Geseke and Brigitte back to Hamburg.

25th November 1942

I am going home for Christmas! Hurrah! How I am looking forward to it! Asta is so childish, always peeved over any small thing. And yet, I have to be careful and remain friendly to her, so that I may be allowed to stay there. In the country there is still much more to eat. People are doing their slaughtering secretly; they wash their

Hilke by the river Alster, winter 1942.

Hilke with our father, winter 1942.

Our parents, Lottie and Curt, at the beginning of 1943.

shoes in milk to make them shiny, and things like that. They should rather give the city people a mouthful of milk! And on top of it all they say, 'It serves the town people right'. Once I am in Hamburg I will help all day long and do what I can. Ah, this is often my only ray of hope! How I look forward to seeing Regine. She was born on October 14th. Mummy had a very easy delivery. In a letter she wishes me the same when my turn comes.

25th January 1943

The Christmas holidays have gone far too quickly. Regine's christening was lovely. Henning was Godfather and held the baby over the christening bowl. The cakes were like in times of peace!

2nd February 1943

At the moment heroic battles near Stalingrad are taking place. Our 6th army is surrounded there. Some sections have surrendered when they ran out of ammunition. The poor fellows! What they have to cope with! We will never see them again! They will be transported to Siberia. The others are still trapped. The heroes defend themselves with sticks, spades and rifle butts. They have eaten up their last horse: will the rest have time to shoot themselves at the last moment?

Unfortunately I have to start writing in Latin script. I find it very hard to change.*

Over time I notice more and more how pessimistic Asta's mother, the Baroness, is. She sometimes listens to the foreign radio station and she also makes butter secretly. Both things are strictly forbidden. When the Bolsheviks arrive she wants to flee with all of us, perhaps to the island of Rügen and from there, in case of emergency, to Sweden. Having earned some money there, she will sell her jewellery and go to South America. All these fantastic plans! Yesterday I heard again on the radio about a big air raid on Hamburg!

Brigitte has been in hospital for more than five weeks with scarlet fever, measles and kidney trouble. Poor girl, she has to be in bed for another three weeks. Henning, who is now 16, has been called

---

* *The first part of the diary was written in Gothic script.*

Left: *Manor House in Waldschwind.*
Right: *Henning climbing a telephone pole on a Home Air Defence exercise, 1943.*

up. He is helping with the news service in Hamburg. He connects telephone calls. Every day they have lessons from a nice captain in the army. The food is not so good. My cousins are in the artillery. That is supposed to be boring. During air raids Henning has to go out to the field telephone, where he sends on the commands.

Asta always says my handwriting is so childlike. How will I write later?

Our house is very long and has only one floor above the ground floor. I like the Baron very much, Asta so-so, but I despise the Baroness. She often makes such tactless remarks, e.g. 'One can know a person by the way he packs a parcel.' Mummy had just sent a badly packed parcel!

8th June 1943

Asta has just started her period, making her even more irritable than normal. In any case it is very difficult to get on with her. Nobody else has stuck it here as long as I have.

Today I have become a teenager: '*Vierzehn Jahre, sieben Wochen, ist der Backfisch ausgekrochen*' (fourteen years and seven weeks the teenager has hatched).

Exactly four weeks after Asta I, too, 'have taken off my childhood's shoes', as Mummy would have said. At the moment I am unwell for the second time in my life.

End of July 1943

These were short and sad holidays. I am back again in Waldschwind, without having seen my parents and siblings for longer than a week, and without finishing all the alterations to my clothes. The whole family has been dispersed. Geseke and Brigitte are in Pomerania on the estate where Geseke was before the holidays. Henning is in Hamburg with the Luftwaffe, Daddy is at home. Mummy and Regine planned to go to Eisenach (Thüringen) to Aunt Dora von Müffling. I don't really know where she is at the moment. Mummy decided in the morning that we should all leave Hamburg. We only had time to pack the most necessary things. At 6 p.m. we went to the Moorweide, a kind of green common. Our hopes to stay together became dashed. Far too little room on one lorry. Without as much as saying 'good-bye' I was put on a lorry with my suitcase and off it went. I could hardly suppress my tears. What became of the others? No idea! In that lorry we drove over lots of broken glass up to the harbour area. It was horrific there. Whole areas of the city had collapsed, burying people underneath.

Along the streets were crying women and unconscious children suffering from terrible burns. The lorry went over a bump. What was that? I saw a charred corpse in the street. Only the bones. In Harburg, a southern suburb of Hamburg, I enquired for the next train to Würzburg, which is the nearest city to Waldschwind. Three hours to wait! Then into an overcrowded train where I had to stand all through the night to Würzburg. Everybody was surprised to see me and everything seems so peaceful here.

Now, a little about the most horrific nights of my life. It started in the night from Saturday to Sunday, 24th–25th July 1943.★

Five minutes after the siren had sounded a terrific shooting started. Then hundreds of bombs fell. The walls were trembling, the light went out. Smash! Three window panes shattered! When we heard the howling of the bombs we covered our ears so that our eardrums wouldn't be damaged. Brigitte and the live-in help cried. During a break in the firing Mummy put on Daddy's steel helmet from the First World War and went upstairs to see whether anything was on fire.

Daddy was in Pomerania to fetch Geseke for the holidays. As Henning was away, too, it meant there was no man in the house. Mummy called 'Fire!' and the cook and I ran upstairs. Luckily it was a false alarm. After the alarm was over the sky was blood red. Fire all around. The wooden door was in splinters, because the lock had been blown out by the pressure of the hot air. I woke up at 9 a.m., but because of all the smoke and dirt it was as dark as if it were 4 a.m. It did not get light all morning. The soot on the trees, on broken glass and on rubble was finger thick, everywhere one looked. Regine's cradle was full of broken glass. All day long the early warning alarm sounded. I didn't get to look at the city. There was no light and no gas, so we had to start the wood burning stove in order to cook a breakfast at noon. In the afternoon Henning came for three hours. It's a miracle that he got through, with no

★ *See also the chapter on St Nikolai church, page 121.*

transport working. He was meant to see whether our house was still standing as telephones were not working. (Is it still standing at this moment?) Terrible when you don't get any news! Where is Mummy? Where Henning is working with the air force, half the helpers' homes have been bombed. The next siren sounded while Henning was still with us. We thought at first it wouldn't get so bad during the day, but nevertheless we went into the cellar. When Henning looked the house next door was on fire, the same that burnt last year. Four canisters – fifty incendiary bombs – were ablaze. The cook and I were helping.

Daddy was still away and Henning had to go back to the Luftwaffe. On one Sunday afternoon so much had happened in our district. Yet, everywhere neighbours were helping one another. The sailors from the barracks behind our house were climbing high up, like daredevils, in order to put out the fire.

After the all-clear I went to the Moorweide to pick grass for my rabbits. I had given two little ones to Brigitte for her birthday. Every two steps an incendiary bomb had hit. Most of them were still smouldering. A policeman came and said I might as well go home and slaughter the rabbits. In the evening I went with Daddy for a walk through the centre of the town. The St Nicolai church is burnt out. Daddy's office was lucky. All around the houses had collapsed like match boxes. All the shops are burnt out, including all our things that we had left with the seamstress, dry-cleaning etc. Among them two winter coats and two brand new dresses of mine. Hardly had we come home when the alarm started again. When it finished at 4 o'clock there was fire everywhere again. At 9 o'clock in the morning the devastation continued. Once the few outer walls of the houses have been blasted away, the city of Hamburg will be flattened. We would have been mad to stay until our house was hit, so we all left Hamburg that evening.

*Firestorm in Hamburg, July 1943. (Courtesy of Eckart
& Messtorff, Hamburg, 1946)*

I shall never forget this terrible experience! In such a mess it is impossible to imagine peace any more. Does this have to happen, that such towns, our beloved homes, are simply being wiped out? An epidemic has broken out in Hamburg. I am worried about Henning; he is still with the air force there. Daddy also remains in Hamburg. Geseke and Brigitte are in Dorow in Pomerania, Mummy and the baby Regine are with Aunt Dora von Müffling, in Eisenach in Thüringen. I am going to visit them tomorrow.

29th October 1943 (Waldschwind near Schweinfurt)

In the meantime there has been an air raid even here. The target was Schweinfurt. 121 shot down. It was on a Thursday. We were just about to go by bike to our confirmation lesson when the Baroness stormed in, very upset. 'You cannot go, Schweinfurt is being attacked, the sky is full of aeroplanes.'

We all ran to the paddock and just managed to see a plane come down in a spin, pulling a trail of smoke behind it. We saw a group of enemy fighters being shot at and shortly afterwards some 25 parachutes were hovering in the air. A bomber exploded in the air and the burning parts were spinning to the ground. Then it seemed too dangerous and the Baroness ordered: 'Everybody into the coal cellar!' Perhaps we would have been just as safe in the wood or in a ditch.

But the Baroness was so excited, that she seemed literally to pull the planes from the sky. According to her, all the planes were crashing on our house, and we were all done for. One did, indeed, come down very close to us. Luckily it stalled and made an emergency landing nearby, right in the middle of a flock of sheep, where the same panic broke out as at home among us. The

Spire and ruins of St Nikolai Church in the centre of Hamburg.

shepherd wanted to take the three soldiers prisoners (the others had parachuted down beforehand), but they pointed their pistols in front of his face and then ran off into the wood. In the surrounding area many planes have come down, all in all 121, and Schweinfurt has suffered much damage to both civilian and business buildings.

The next day we inspected the four-engined bomber. There was a great deal of ammunition for the machine-guns. Everything was very interesting, but very little room for eight people. The bomber was covered with shot holes; one of the propellers was missing. A pin-up woman in a bathing suit had been painted on the outside. I found everything fascinating. For the first time I had seen planes come down.

In July Daddy's office was burnt out. Apart from our furniture and a carpet etc., we also kept jewellery there. The latter, however, could be saved, as it was in a safe. Now Daddy has his office in our house on the ground floor in the Klopstockstraße.

31st January 1944, at the boarding school on Lake Constance

In the Christmas holidays I told my parents again that I really did not like being in Waldschwind any more. Now there are other related children there, so Asta would not be on her own. In short, I had been made to feel by everyone that I was not needed any more. Now Mummy has enrolled me in a German Boarding School near Constance. Surprisingly we heard that they still had a place, so now I have been here for two weeks. In Hegne [on the bank of Lake Constance] is a big main building [previously the Hegne Monastery]. Here, opposite the island Reichenau, is the village Reichenau with many, many houses. It used to be a mental institution, therefore many things are still quite funny, for instance you can only switch on the light with a key. Now it is a National Political Educational College for boys. There are 160 boys in all. As many houses were still empty the Heimschule for Girls has taken over some. We are 80 girls here, but in spite of this there is still much room and many houses are still empty (a shame when you think of the shortage of living accommodation).

Henning and Hilke, winter 1944.

Geseke and Regine, winter 1944.

I am in the Secondary School in the 5th year. Everything is very regimented here. At first I was quite unhappy. Everything was strange, unheated and nothing was prepared. You have to make up your own bed, and get hold of a bedside table, a chair etc. At table you only have rusty-looking cutlery. People are nice but simple. How different from Mummy's former boarding school! But we have to be grateful to have found accommodation that is safe from air attacks. I am learning more here than in Waldschwind.

I have a weekly three-hour period in laundry and three hours of cookery, but also a daily Latin lesson. Food is good considering it is wartime. In the morning three slices of bread and jam, sometimes with butter. For lunch soup, otherwise dessert, like apples or apple purée. A lot of vegetables and always varied. Every Sunday a drink of cocoa; this is really meant only for younger children.

26th February 1944

Against all expectations we have air raids here, too. When they want to fly into southern Germany they fly over Switzerland and then all the pupils have to go into the cellar. This week it was particularly bad. Three times per night and two to three times per day. In the morning the first two lessons are dropped. I don't write this home because Mummy and Daddy would worry as I have come here to avoid the bombings. The food is not so good any more – new brooms sweep clean.

31st May 1944

Now the Easter holidays are long over. I was confirmed on April 2nd. It will be a beautiful memory for a long time. It was a pity that no godparents were there, and Geseke and Brigitte were missing, too. In the morning at 9 o'clock we had the confirmation ceremony in the little St John's Church. My quotation from the Bible was: 'I will bless you, and you shall be a blessing.' At midday we had visitors, and in the evening we had a dinner. Daddy gave a speech, which I will keep. I cried a bit. But it was very beautiful. I was sad when Daddy said, 'Now you say a symbolic good-bye to your childhood.'

Ostern 1944 in Planten u. Blomen.

Hilke with our mother in 'Planten un Blomen', Easter 1944.

The days over Whitsun were absolutely wonderful. We went by boat across Lake Constance to Lindau and Bregenz. Once we missed the boat, so we had to spend the night in a youth hostel. We went on foot. For the first time I saw the Alps close up. Across the water in Switzerland there was snow and I was roasting in the sun! Lovely!

1st June 1944

Sometimes I think that I am so different from most girls of my age. Perhaps I am too much a Hamburg girl, too stiff to make friends easily. I can never find a real girl friend. Still, I now have a good relationship with Schuschi and Putzi, two reasonably nice girls from North Germany.

6th June 1944

I have heard that last night the invasion started. English air force landing troops have landed in northern France. At last, the long-awaited day has arrived! And how differently the news is received just in our class. One girl, whose brother is near the Channel, lies on her bed and cries. Others are up in the air cheering and shouting 'Hurrah'! I cannot do that at the moment. True, I am glad that this endless waiting has now come to an end, but on the whole my mood is solemn. I wonder what is going to happen next. If things go badly, we in Hamburg are not miles away from where the action is. Mummy is in Thüringen with Brigitte at the moment, Regine with Dr Kröll, Daddy's partner and Regine's godfather, in Hamburg. Geseke is still in Pomerania. So, everybody is scattered all over the place.

Our mother with Regine, spring 1944.

8th June 1944

Yesterday we pupils were helping with the harvest on a farm quite near to the border. The way there on a boat was glorious. On the farm we had to work really hard. A large field with radishes had to be done and it was raining as well! In between we had tea and three slices of bread. Real country bread with lard and salami. The return trip was the best. Without rain on an open lorry, down steep wooded paths, zooming round the bends at speed into the valley of Lake Constance. Today we were stiff all over.

16th June 1944

Yesterday I had a letter from Uncle Herbert and Aunt Erika inviting me to visit them in the Black Forest. They are there on holiday and I will go just for a weekend. At last I will get to see the Black Forest. I have always wanted to go there. The dark forest is best, like in the Harz. The train arrives in four hours. Hurrah! I can't wait!

19th June 1944

So, now I have come down again into this 'miserable place' – it really was lovely! Because of a change in the timetable I went the wrong way and so arrived at Badenweiler only around midnight.

Aunt Erika met me from the train and in the guest house I met Uncle Herbert. He is really very small and is limping a bit after his illness. In the guest house I was called Fräulein Hilke for the first time. Carpets, warm water, service, everything was strange after the regimented life at school. The food was good, though we were short of ration tokens. Unfortunately it rained, but we nevertheless did some lovely walks, for instance to the 'Old Man', a high rock with a lovely view to the Vogesen mountains and to the 'Sulphur Cave', a very deep gorge with steam. I was quite sad when I had to leave again. Where will I see Uncle Herbert and Aunt Erica again? Well, let us look forward to the summer holidays in 36 days.

24th June 1944

Today we were allowed to go into town. The film was very nice. For once not just a love story without any depth. I do quite like detective stories, though. Unfortunately! But it's not my fault that I am still so immature and like to read light books. I am a bit embarrassed about it and read them only secretly.

But now to the Summer Solstice. This long-awaited summer feast was from Wednesday to Thursday. Because of rain it was put back by a day.

Wednesday: at 9 o'clock there was a ceremony at school. It lasted until 12 o'clock and was about eastern Germany. After lunch we had an hour's rest, during which I had a letter from Aunt Erika. She had heard about a big air raid on Hamburg. So, of course, during the afternoon I was worried. However, I pulled myself together during the celebration and joined in properly. For the first time I quite liked folk dancing. All the girls were bare footed and dancing in their colourful dirndls to the music. Then we had floor exercises, Punch and Judy, fairytale plays, ball games etc. The evening meal was at 9 p.m., at sunset. Then we marched to the edge of Lake Constance. One could see the Alps very clearly. We lit the pile of wood and sang: 'Rise ye flames'. We had readings and wreaths were thrown into the flames for our fallen heroes. Then our headmistress gave a speech. I felt quite moved, and I swore to be a real help to Mummy, even if we should now lose everything. On Thursday morning we had the sports races. I ran the 75m race in 11.1 seconds; I jumped 3.70 to 3.92m in the long jump, and 105cm in the high jump. I threw almost 6m in the shot put and 28m in rounders ball.

For lunch we had bread-pudding made with rye bread. Then we had the swimming races. I was one of the best (50m in 0.59 seconds). Then we had our rounders game. It finished with a cheer of *zicke-zacke, zicke-zacke heu, heu, heu*! A cross-country run with a thunderstorm rounded off this beautiful and special day.

In the meantime I received my first red express card from Daddy in Hamburg: a 'we-are-alive' card from the family.

The express card sent to Hilke after a severe air raid on Hamburg saying that her family was still alive.

30th June 1944

At night in bed there is always an awful lot of noise. Recently at midnight one of the matrons came in: 'Everybody out of bed and get dressed! Make your beds, turn the mattresses, back into bed and out again!' After that it was quiet. But today we couldn't sleep again with all the noise. The headmistress said yesterday, that every set should have its own specialism. L15 is walking, O6 has sport, we want health and swimming. For that I want to do an exam on Friday. I am rather unprepared at the moment, but I can always try. I hope I'll make it.

End of July 1944

It is almost a month ago that I passed the life-saving test. I am very proud of that. Conditions: diving and swimming under water for 17m, in 3m deep water; picking up two bricks one after another; 15 minutes swimming on your front and 10 minutes swimming on your back without moving your arms while being sprayed with artificial rain; then life-saving for 30m showing the various grips. Give a talk on resuscitation with practical demonstrations.

How I have looked forward to the holidays and now they will soon be over. My report was as follows:

German 3; History 2 (favourite subject); Gymnastics 3; Mathematics 3; English 4; Latin 4; Chemistry 4; Biology 3; Physics 3. I find Latin hardest.

Now something about our wonderful summer holidays. We had rented two rooms in Medingen near Ülzen [about 50 miles south of Hamburg]. As the Conrad's house did not have any domestic help I had to do a lot. The food was nothing special and that is enough reason for Mummy and Frau Mantur, the landlady, to be like cat and mouse! Yet it would have been so nice if we could have gone there again for Christmas away from Hamburg. The walks in the evenings were lovely. Medingen is a small place in the middle of the Lüneburger Heide. Every Sunday Daddy came to visit us and once Henning came, too. That Sunday was the first and only day for two years when the whole family was together. So, of course, we took some photographs.

Geseke and Brigitte, that is a problem. I always look forward to seeing them and then it turns into a big disappointment.

Twice I went home from Medingen to Hamburg. The first time I stayed for three days. I couldn't get back earlier because

Our father with Hilke, Geseke and Brigitte.

Hilke with baby Regine in Medingen, summer 1944.

Our mother, Lottie, 1945.

Left to right: Lottie, Henning, Geseke, Hilke, Regine, Curt and Brigitte in about 1946, when the whole family was reunited.

the bridges over the Elbe had been destroyed. I had to travel because of the seamstress coming to alter our clothes. In the evening I went with Daddy to the Fährhaus café, Ratskeller Restaurant or to relations. I entertained Aunt Elise for an hour and I also went to the Sagebiel Restaurant. With Daddy alone by the Elbe! The first time since before Waldschwind! The second time I went for a day to Hamburg with Geseke. We had to change trains five times because of the bridges.

The 2½-week holiday was soon over. I took Brigitte back to Thüringen and went on to Constance. It took me from Monday until Thursday, two nights without sleeping. We were stuck in

Bebra from 12 until 4 due to an air-raid warning. I missed the train because of over-crowding. At 8 o'clock we had a full alarm in Erfurt, and on top of that I lost Brigitte in a strange town. At 12 o'clock we continued our journey and at 2 o'clock we reached Oberhof [a little spa near Eisenach]. Then we really got lost and only arrived at Brigitte's children's home at 5 o'clock. The next day they had their very first bombs of the war. In the evening I said good-bye. It was quicker than with Mummy, when I just couldn't hide a few tears. A quick kiss and Brigitte was off without even turning round! I went to the cinema and then through the wood to the station. There I wrote a letter home until 1 o'clock in the early morning. Then off by express train to Constance! I didn't even unpack my things, but instead the next morning I was up immediately to help with the harvest on the same farm near the border as in June 1944. So, here I have been for over a week now, staying until Friday. The food is excellent, but it is very, very hard work. There are four of us. We sleep on straw with blankets. We work from 6 a.m. until 10 p.m. with only a few breaks. It is exhausting. I hold on to Mummy's words saying, 'Everything will pass … after every November May will come again'. In political matters as well, only we are not sure whether there will indeed be a May again after November. Now the Americans (from the invasion) have already reached Paris. Terrible! In the east the Russians are at the big bend of the River Weichsel. And to think that once we were in Stalingrad! The 'total war' has been intensified. New rules: no holidays at all for anybody. Does that mean I won't get home for Christmas? That is the only thing that keeps my head above water. Henning will get home in order to go to a camp to toughen up young people. Daddy has been told to do other work, and Mummy will soon know whether she has to go to work, too. Our young nanny has been enlisted in the war effort and soon the cook will follow.

Hilke in the summer of 1944.

2nd September 1944

Recently Verdun has fallen. They are getting nearer and nearer. Yesterday I came back from harvest duty. In two days school is starting again and with it horrible Latin! During my absence pupils had to move and I can't find my belongings anywhere. Here a sock and there a book, things like that. The school has expanded and taken in younger children; young pupils are everywhere. Utter chaos!

4th September 1944

So, here we are! I can hardly believe it and yet today the school has been suspended! The headmistress spoke about the serious situation and told us that all over Germany schools are closing.

We will have to go back to our duties for the Fatherland. Now I don't need to learn the Latin vocabulary for tomorrow. What will happen to my *Abitur* [A-level exam]? What will I be one day? A charwoman? Today should have been the first day of the new term. One more year and I would have reached my 'finishing-off' qualification, the same as Mummy. Now that has all been suspended.

I have been home again for a week now. We are supposed to do our 'service' at home. My parents were, of course, flabbergasted, when I suddenly appeared for lunch. I couldn't warn them beforehand, because we had to be away from school within two days, taking all our belongings. We spent all day packing up. In the evening we had a farewell celebration. The worst thing about it was that I couldn't get rid of my huge suitcase, as it seemed that parcels and suitcases could no longer be sent on separately. However, I did manage it in the end, although I still had to carry five pieces of luggage myself. After a six-hour delay I arrived in Hamburg. I registered immediately at the employment exchange. However, surprise, surprise, they didn't even want me. They said I should go back to school. The schools here are still open. So things are different here from what we were told down there. Daddy has enrolled me at my previous school which has now moved to an area between Hamburg and Berlin and is housed in a collection point camp. This means I won't be staying at home for very long. Of course, should the Hegne school re-open I would rather go back there. Well, we will see.

Henning is going to the 'toughening-up' camp tomorrow for three weeks. Daddy has to work in armaments. There is often an alarm. The enemy is very near Aachen. Uncle Herbert and Aunt Erika left Rheydt voluntarily. Officially people are not yet told to leave home. However, everybody thinks that there will be an invasion in north-west Germany by Cuxhaven or in Holstein. Terrible! So near to us!

18th October 1944

In spite of the political situation we are back at school in Hegne by Lake Constance. While the school authorities were sorting out the muddle, I was only too glad to stay at home for five weeks. As Mummy was ill again I helped a lot with Regine. Often we went to get some fruit from round about Hamburg. Mummy taught me some Latin, but, unfortunately, we didn't get very far, as the order came to return to school again. The cases were packed in a rush and off I went! Now I have been here for four days. I like the community and I feel more settled now. Perhaps that is because of my friendship with Annelotte Bock. Our stream has been thinned out, based on the girls' character and behaviour, and is becoming something of a showpiece under the guidance of our new leader Mrs Kohlmeier. She is very nice and forceful.

19th November 1944

We are already getting on with making Christmas presents. Where I shall be for my holidays is not yet certain.

29th January 1945

I spent the short Christmas holidays in Hamburg. The journey took fifty-six hours. Henning is in Denmark in an army health corps, where he gets very good food. He often sends bacon and sausages. Regine has made great progress with talking. She and I were the only ones at home for Christmas, as the others didn't come.

Daddy is still working as a harbour worker with Blohm & Voss, at the shipyard, as part of the home defence.

Here in Reichenau we have no heating, so we stay in the main house in Hegne over Easter. I am often hungry. We are not allowed to wash anything ourselves, although I have my own washing powder. I think that's scandalous. We had a twenty-day-long cookery course. I am quite a good cook now and look forward to the next holidays, when I will do the cooking myself. I hope our house will still be there.

There are no express trains any more, and we can no longer write letters. I am often in despair as I can't get any ration tokens or mending yarn sent to me.

In the east the Russians are now on German soil. They are outside Königsberg and Schneidemühl, Thorn and Posen. In spite of the serious situation we continue with our dancing lessons, only for girls, of course. I used to find the whole thing disgusting, so I walked out. But then they danced the tango in such a common way. Now I love dancing the polka, waltzes, folk dances and the contra.

8th February 1945

Annelotte is ill with scarlet fever. She is in hospital. Our stream has to live in the cellar for ten days, separate from the others. We don't have many lessons, but we have a lot of fresh air. We now sleep in bunk beds. One can work in peace and quiet.

At table I hardly eat any more and it is hard for me even to turn up. Oh, why should I always have such an unhappy love? And when I do feel love, I am never allowed to show it. By now I have learnt a bit more how to control my feelings and I don't think that I have let the person involved become aware of them. But then again, in some way she is really my first love. At least I know now that there are still people whom I like in every way; whom I understand totally, even in religious matters. At last I have regained my Protestant faith. In a way I feel I have been confirmed a year too early. Here at school almost nobody is a mainstream Christian and because I don't really have an idea of Christ as such, I thought that I was basically like the others, a believer in God. I see in Christ a symbol or an image, like so many others in the Catholic Church. Now, one of my teachers, Fräulein D., says that one is in fact a Christian if one believes in some higher being, if one has a deep trust and if one prays. Well, this is the case with me. I think some of the 'believers in God' are basically Christian, but do not call themselves so because the word 'Christian' is unfashionable in Hitler's Germany. The church, where I only go at Christmas, is supposed to revitalise our faith. Nevertheless, we can see our true church in nature. This resonates with me totally. So there is, after all, still someone who is exactly like me. Fräulein D. is rather tall and looks to be of Westphalian origin.

There are different kinds of love: 1 the love of the soul of a person; 2 his or her actions; 3 his or her body.

With me and Fräulein D. the first one applies. I also love her music, even though I can't play any music myself. She is also like me in the way she dresses. Is that how love for a fiancée feels? I don't know, at any rate, she is the first person I should like to marry. I love and worship her. One day, when I read these lines again, will I still understand myself or will I smile and say: 'Puppy love'?

8th March 1945

The following has made me wonder whether or not to write it in this diary. After all one is supposed to write the good and the not so good things about oneself.

Yesterday I asked Fräulein D. what she thought of the quotation: 'For the greater a man, the more forgiving he is in his anger', for I never quite understood this. One cannot forgive everything, one has one's pride. She replied: 'Of course one has one's pride, for instance one should not "run after" someone else. Yet one should always try to be forgiving. It would be petty to stick to one's hurt pride.' (See novel *Michael Kohlhaas* by Kleist.) One should think of the greater good. She mentioned when Bismarck was reconciled with the Prussian King, later Kaiser Wilhelm, who had been so short-sighted when he wanted to march into Vienna, which would have destroyed all Bismarck's political efforts. With regard to the concept 'Love your enemies' her view was to relate this mainly to one's personal enemies, not to the political ones. One should respect the enemy and forgive him, also for one's own sake. A mother loves her child, however naughty. That is nothing new. But there are few people besides Jesus who can forgive their biggest enemy, and these men then have done something really great. Did she want to say that I shouldn't run after her? Or was she really only referring to my question. And yet she continues to be so kind to me, that I find a farewell difficult. But then I had decided a while ago to avoid showing my feelings. Still she remains in my heart.

12th March 1945

Yesterday we had a wonderful commemorative service for our fallen heroes. At first Fräulein D. played the Funeral March by Beethoven, my favourite piano piece. Then the headmistress spoke.

The whole service was quite Christian. It included the hymns: 'Now thank we all our God' and 'A mighty stronghold is our God'. I notice how everybody in times of need looks to God. Frau Dr W. said, 'You have learnt to include death in your lives;

that is to say, you know that you could die at any moment. Therefore you are deep inside yourselves prepared for death.'

18th April 1945

In the last few weeks we had a DRK [German Red Cross] course. Yesterday I passed the examination as a DRK helper with 'good'. Immediately afterwards we got the news that we had to leave in three hours. For weeks we had been prepared for this, and so I coped quite well. Two woollen blankets, a briefcase, a lunch box and a suitcase. I put on seven lots of underwear, three pairs of stockings and three dresses. That should be sufficient. I also packed my certificates. But money is another thing. That is really bad. The school gave me 30 Reichsmark as an advance. Everyone who had acquaintances in unoccupied areas of Germany had to go. I went with my friend, Annelotte Bock, to someone she knows here in Oberstdorf. Ingeborg came with us. We hope to get some sort of work soon, perhaps in a hospital. We have to stand on our own two feet now and especially earn some money.

It is glorious here in the mountains. This is the first time that I am actually living in the Alps. During the train journey we saw many injured people. Often they had been travelling for a fortnight and had only paper bandages on their wounds. If only I were already working in a hospital!

Overleaf: *Diary entries, April 1945.*

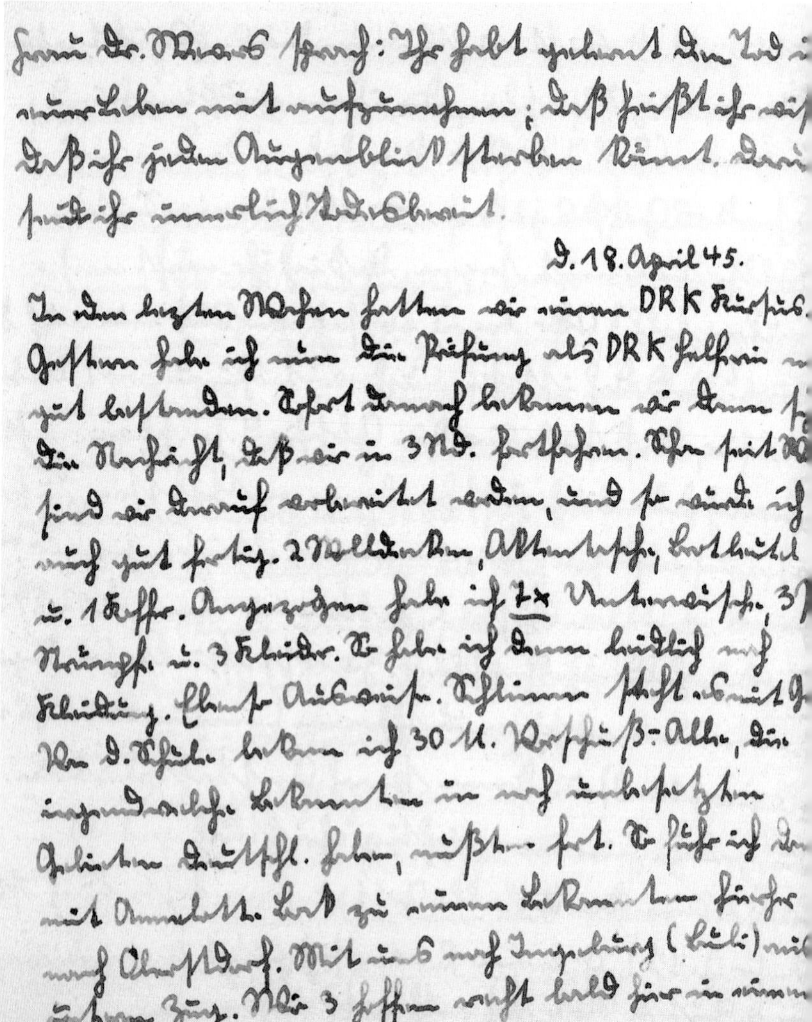

D. 18. April 45.

…er einem Lazarett im Einsatz zu kommen. Denn
wir müssen ja jetzt auf eigenen Beinen stehen und
…er selbst Geld verdienen. – Hier in dem Lager ist es
herrlich. (Es ist ja das 1.x, daß ich in d. Alpen wohne) Der
…ft ist nicht so sehr schlimm u. auch nicht viel. Den
…g sehen wir schon viele Verwundete. Die waren oft
Tage unterwegs u. nur mit Papierverbänden
…sorgt. Oh, wenn ich nur erst im Einsatz wäre! –

d. 22. April 1945.

In Oberstdorf waren wir nun beim
Oberstabsarzt, welcher uns aber nicht nehmen, weil
wir zu jung seien. Annelotte bleibt vorläufig bei
ihren Bekannten u. Ingeburg u. ich haben uns in
…stadt beim Gebiet gemeldet. Jetzt sind wir
mit … hier in Langenwang bei Oberstdorf in
einem kl. KLV Lager von 30 Mädchen. (13–14 jährige)
Doch bleiben wir hier nicht lange, weil wir hier ja
nicht viel helfen können. Hoffentl. kommen wir
als Gesundheitsdienstmädel in ein größeres Lager.
Natürlich wollen wir eigentl. nicht, sondern Einsatz.

22nd April 1945

In Oberstdorf we went to see the captain of the medical corps, who did not accept us, however, because we were too young. Annelotte is going to stay with her acquaintances for the time being, and Ingeborg and I have registered with the local council. Since yesterday we have been in a small KLV [Children's Evacuation to the Country] camp for thirty girls here, aged thirteen to fourteen. However, we are not going to stay for long, as we are not able to help very much. I hope we can get into a bigger camp as some sort of nursing assistants. We don't want lessons, of course, we want to be of service.

I had quite a nice sixteenth birthday. Though I had no news from home, I had kept my last year's birthday letter from Mummy. This year it was even more appropriate in terms of content. As a treat I went on my first mountain walk with gentian and wild crocuses.

Now the enemy is already in Lüneburg. What might they do at home? And Brigitte is in Thüringen, probably in the hands of the enemy. Here they are getting nearer and nearer, too. 100km away.

Letter from Mummy for my 15th Birthday, April 1944:

Dear Hilke,

For your fifteenth birthday we wish you all the best. In these hard times there is not much happiness around! But I hope that even the hard times, the separation from the family and the other difficulties of life, will turn out for your good, and make you into a hardworking, modest and undemanding person.

For you many things that we took for granted will bring happiness: such as having enough clothes, food and drink. You certainly are not spoilt, but the industriousness and energy to get on in life, which our grandparents had in such high degree, is missing in your generation.

These qualities have got lost in the easy pre-war years. But you must let them come out again from your heritage. You have, just like our grandparents, early independence. They, however, combined it with that reverence and deep respect for tradition, which is lacking in young people today. Not so much with you, but with Henning I noticed for instance how he spoke of Uncle Carl-Ludwig who was President of the Chamber of Commerce and a man of great experience and wisdom, in a not very respectful manner. Such people have sacrificed a great deal, by their own free will in order to succeed in life.

Enfolding you in my arms in true love,
Your Mummy.

25th April 1945

Today in this area all the papers have been burnt. All the pictures of Hitler are being buried, the flags torn to bits. Yes, I can understand all that, thus they will be saved from desecration, but to desecrate yourself, like our housekeeper here, never!

Today we had to dry our dishes with the swastika flag. I couldn't stand that and so I walked out.

Alas, I will gladly bear anything, if only I know that I will see my siblings and parents again. Hamburg is now surrounded. I don't know whether they are fighting in the streets. In any case I don't know exactly where the enemy is now, for we can no longer listen to the news of our armed forces and the newspapers don't have any information either. We are getting more and more hungry. People are queuing for three hours in front of the baker's and then they fight over the few loaves that are still available. We have ration tokens but no bread or flour. Here in the Allgäu there is no agriculture and the other areas are occupied. So we live on cheese, which they do have here. Every day we have low-flying aircraft shooting. And it will get worse and worse. We must not think any more, merely work instead, like a machine. I am now all alone in foreign lands. Oh, I do reproach Mummy and myself. Years ago I said, the worst thing is, to be separated from your family. Nevertheless Mummy and Daddy insisted that I should stay down here in the south in any event, and not, as I had intended, go home at the last minute. If only I had done so after all. Now I am all alone, completely at the mercy of the black people here in the French zone. However, I am not altogether blameless, because Mummy had told me to stay in the larger community and not to try and save myself on my own. And what did I do? The opposite. But when the school turned us out on the street I had no time to think and I forgot Mummy's orders. Now the enemy is by Lake Constance and Constance itself has been put under Red Cross protection. If only I had stayed there. But the communities, the KLV camp and our school, had been disbanded by their leaders! We were told to go to friends and that we should take other girls with us. That's why Annelotte asked me to come along. That's how it is: one person says 'Stay together', another 'Go your separate ways'. Not surprising that I didn't know what to do. But then again, nobody would have known what to do. So, best to wait and see, stoically, and to hope that one is lucky, or at best think of God. There is heavy fighting in Berlin. The Führer is still there.

28th April 1945

As the present KLV Camp has been disbanded, I am again on the street. As from tomorrow there is nothing to eat here any more and the children have to find accommodation by themselves. Having no food is the worst of it. Here in the Allgäu there are no potatoes and no cereals. The stocks have gone and supplies are not available. The mayor said there would be a revolution. In eight days one wouldn't be able to get a slice of bread any more. For the last few days we have lived on soup and boiled nettles, which give you trouble in your intestines, of course.

Yesterday Ingeborg and I went from house to house, to inns and farms like beggars, in order to find work, accommodation and food. Everywhere we told people about our misfortune and asked whether they might need a live-in help, nanny, cleaning woman or kitchen girl. At long last I found a place with an old woman. I am supposed to start tomorrow. She is old and ill, yet her daughter-in-law doesn't look after her. I wonder what the place is like. But then, she is not a farmer, so it won't be much better as far as food is concerned. We must wait and see!

The day before yesterday I witnessed a terrible low-altitude air raid. Five minutes after the siren sounded eleven enemy fighter planes came down quite low and shot at the villages and country roads with weapons they had on board. I was just crossing a bridge and quickly hid in the bushes by the embankment, absolutely flat on the ground. The air raid lasted for half an hour. My face firmly pressed into the soil, I heard the bullets hit their targets. Finally only the odd bursts of fire and then we could walk on. On our way we saw six dead horses, one injured horse and one dead farmer lying on the road. Proper war. Sometimes we live like gods in France, and then we are hungry again. Recently we found a few American cans. We ate and devoured the ham, the cream, pudding etc. until we felt sick. Today we are so hungry we can hardly walk.

2nd May 1945

In Oberstdorf where I had found accommodation, new residents cannot have ration cards. So I had to move on into the Walser Valley. There I went to a KLV woman doctor, who sent me to Birgsau, three hours from Oberstdorf, as a DRK helper. Finally, after almost three weeks on the road, I have found a more permanent shelter. The food is very good and I have my own room. There are thirty twelve-year-old boys, whose socks I am mending, and I help with other things. Ingeborg is in a camp nearby. I also help in another camp, but I live here in Birgsau.

Yesterday, 1st May, we had a lot of snow. The enemy has advanced with tanks into Oberstdorf, just when I was actually walking to Birgsau. But because the hospital town surrendered immediately, the tanks turned round. Every cowshed has hung out a white flag. The occupational forces are different from what I had thought. Actually, I haven't seen an enemy face to face yet. May God grant that no harm comes to me and that I can get home in two months.

6th May 1945

As I do not write letters home any more, I feel the need to write in my diary more often. I am totally cut off from the world up here, among thirty boys with whom I hardly talk. They are all so young and I have to mend socks all day long. Terrible to have neither radio nor newspaper! I would absolutely love to hear how things are at home, whether I can possibly catch a train again and so on. For this much is clear: home as soon as possible. Perhaps another three weeks waiting and then with this camp up to Stuttgart; and then from there on my own to Hamburg. I hope there will be an opportunity to travel one way or another.

Today I went for a walk. The snow has gone and I found so many flowers that I didn't know. The food is quite good up here. But I only get three meals, so I do feel hungry.

Ascension Day 1945

This year we celebrate Ascension Day again. Göbbels has poisoned himself with his family. The Führer is dead. Apparently the armistice document has been signed already. In the last few days I saw French occupation troops several times, nosing around the farm here. They demanded beer and fried eggs. All cameras had to be handed in. Nobody is allowed to go by bicycle and there is a curfew from 8 p.m. until 6 a.m. The telephone is disconnected, and it is forbidden to have a meeting of more than three people. This is all trivial at this stage. Oh Lord, I wonder whether there will again be such huge reparation costs as after the First World War. I so look forward to getting home, but there the trouble will start in a different way: currency devaluation etc. Who would have expected such an end – and six years of fighting for nothing.

In the last few days I have been homesick for Regine. When I see her again she will be three years old and I will have missed her sweet 'growing-up' period. With the Mittlere Reife [first public examination in secondary school] I have now reached a certain level in my school education. But I have no idea what I want to be one day. In a way it is time that I think about that; but at the moment my one and only aim is 'Hamburg, home, my family'.★

★ *The diary now continues in an ordinary exercise book that cannot be locked.*

Diary entry, May 1945.

May 1945, KLV Camp Birgsau near Oberstdorf (East of Lake Constance)

Now my old faithful friend, the diary, is full, and I have to start a new one. This will not be a wartime diary, like the old one, but there will be more than enough hard times to come.

I will have to leave behind many treasured keepsakes and precious things when I leave for Hamburg! But the diaries are coming with me. What a pity that I cannot lock this.

Ever more cars with occupation troops zoom up here. The boys like to rush to the windows or even shake hands with the enemy. Pfui! I just stare at the crowded cars, and still cannot believe it. First 'Hosanna, hosanna!', and then 'Crucify him!'

One of the Hitler Youth Group leaders said yesterday that the enemy radio station reported more truths than ours did. He wouldn't have dared say that six months ago. Every stable boy is free to utter his political opinion in a loud voice. They know damn all! Yesterday I heard that Austria is meant to become a monarchy. The land east of the Elbe will be Russian Hamburg as well? But I cannot believe that the English and Americans would give the harbour to the Russians. That would be awful. Then I might not be able to get home! [In the event Hamburg was not fought over because, luckily, the mayor, Kaufmann, surrendered the city to the British Army against Hitler's orders, doubtless risking his life.]

Whitsun Sunday 1945

Today is Whitsun and also Mothering Sunday. Like all the other years, this year, too, I picked a little bunch of forget-me-nots. Only that is now on my bedside table.

I have packed my new rucksack, for I think this is the last Sunday here. The director of the camp, too, wants to get away from here and is growing more and more impatient.

26th May 1945 – Beginning of the big journey

So, once again we are on the road, that is to say, at the moment in a rain sodden wood near Kempten.

For days everybody in the camp had packed their rucksacks and waited for the lorry, which was meant to take us to Ulm. Today, all of a sudden, it came and off we went. But, already, in Kempten the Americans gave us a problem because of the French passes. But we don't want to go back, because 1) as from Monday nobody is allowed to leave Oberstdorf and 2) there is no more food up there. Therefore we are sitting here in the wood, hoping to get through tomorrow.

27th May 1945

We slept overnight in two barns in the hay. The first night in hay for me. I slept brilliantly, just a little cold. Today we are sunbathing in the meadow and making plans. We still have provisions. I am thinking of Daddy because it is his birthday today. Towards the west the road is blocked. Therefore the thirty-six boys may have to wait here with local farmers. That may mean that I have to go on my pilgrimage on my own, whilst the way to the north is still free. The farmers here are quite different.

One can spend the night anywhere and we even got some milk (10 litres per 15 people). I will stay here with farmers until tomorrow, then hopefully have a pass to get to Augsburg where I will wait for a car. As long as I have enough money I will travel. When it runs out I will work for a wage and on it goes… It is hard nowadays for a girl to get from one corner of Germany to the other.

In the afternoon

In the meantime I have separated from the boys. They want to go from here towards the west on foot.

How they can do that without a pass I don't know. But it is not my business any more. The farewell was actually a little hard. Many boys had to leave some of their luggage behind. The farmers' wives are, of course, more than happy after six years of war to get some good coats and trousers for their children. In return the boys are given bread, cheese and milk. Well, I will have to do the same when I have no more money and food. Oh, if only Mummy knew!

1st June 1945

It is already June, now! Oh dear, will I be home in August? The two to three days here have been quite nice. But the farmers are very poor, so I will have to go. One day I went in vain to Kempten hurrying from travel agent to the nutrition office, to the occupation headquarters to the mayor. But to no avail! The Americans do not want to give me a pass. [To get from the French zone in the south to the British zone in the north you had to pass through the American zone.] There is still too big a crowd. All evacuees want to get home as soon as possible. That means being patient! By chance I met a girl from Hamburg. She offered me accommodation with a friend, Frau Meyer, for three days. The bed was good, the food as well, but the place was a pigsty. The work was not too hard, but the man was a poor day-labourer. Because of the rain, I had trousers on, just like Mummy at Aunt Dora's. Everything was very small. The dog licked the plates after the meal, which were afterwards rinsed in cold water. A dirty cloth completed the washing up. Hundreds of flies. In short, everything stank sour and the waste bin in the flat, which was terribly dirty, was not emptied for days. Well, I must say, I was glad yesterday, when I found a farmer nearby, who can take me on for two to three weeks as a helper with the harvest. I wangled it quite well saying that I had to leave Frau Meyer.

It is much nicer here. I share my room with two other harvest helpers, who have also been to a grammar school. The food is not so good, but then the work is not quite so hard. The people are really kind and show understanding. I am quite suntanned and, of course, dead tired. I hope they are not as hungry in Hamburg. Apparently there is no more bread for ordinary people here. To make matters worse they are short of potatoes and cereals have run out, too. One cannot get rid of the ration tokens for meat because there is none. Oh dear!

3rd June 1945

Newspapers and radio have not been available for a long time and we don't hear much about political matters. I don't know whether to believe in Hitler's death, especially as no corpse has been found. The real Hitler was the great idealist, but the many little Hitlers, the Party big shots, have betrayed him. The great ideas of Hitler cannot be denied. The main mistakes came from the many little Führer-upstarts.★

Although the enemies are behaving themselves reasonably well, especially the Americans, every day there are new incidents of rape from the side of the Moroccans. A French officer said: 'We had

★ *Hilke's school, originally a private Catholic school, had been taken over by the National-Socialist Party in order to indoctrinate the pupils with the new 'Nazi' ideas. See the section on the Deutsche Heimschule, page 117.*

to promise the Moroccans a German woman so that they would fight at all.' The Poles and concentration camp people are also very dangerous. They raid the farms and demand wine in the inns.

6th June 1945

The farmer's wife here has the same way of speaking as Aunt Martha, except for the dialect. Yesterday we got the first cart load of hay in. My word! What a job! If only I were home. For the first time I got badly sunburnt on my neck and arms. That's the trouble: I go red, but not brown.

8th June 1945

The sunburn gets worse and worse. My arms are full of little blisters, which hurt, of course. I have no cream, which might help a bit. The work is very, very hard, especially in the evening at 8 o'clock when the hay on the carts needs to be loaded off. The hay radiates such heat. To sleep there just one night would mean certain death. My feet are burning and my knee is hurting again. Because of the heavy bales I have probably ruined my abdomen as I often feel pain and tiredness there. But what can I do? Work is heavy everywhere!

10th June 1945

Why didn't Mummy send me a telegram around Easter that I should come home? I ask myself that all the time. Haven't I always hinted in my letters that at such times all children belong with their parents? Now I sit here alone in the world and don't hear about anything. How long will that last? Soon I will have been in the Allgäu for two months and it was bad for me nearly everywhere. I left Lake Constance with thirty Marks and now I have double the amount. I get ten Marks per week here; including this week I have seventy Marks.

16th June 1945

Now I have been with this farmer for two weeks. Yesterday all men over sixteen years of age had to register with the French authorities. We women on our own were very afraid that during this time the French or Poles would come to raid everywhere. I hid my things in the hay. But luckily nothing happened. Here we are very close to the border between the French and the American zones. They often pick men up off the field and move them to France for re-building work. I hope the French and Americans agree soon as to which part of the land should go to whom, then I might get an opportunity to leave. Apparently there are trains again from Kempten to Augsburg. I wonder whether ordinary people can use them.

1st July 1945

Today I have been here for exactly one month. Tomorrow I will go again to Kempten, 12km away, to see whether they will give me a pass. Today it is two months since I said goodbye to Ingeborg (my last friend) at the crossroad Spielmansau–Birgsau. I had predicted that we would never see each other again and that has turned out to be the case. When things get hard, one is alone.

For a few days now I have had a very nice almost spiritual time with two other girls. They have a 40-year-old friend, whom we visit. We are read to or shown some pictures. The 'friend' is called Fräulein Schmidt and she paints. In the evening I often pick cherries and the next day I have tummy ache. But the worst is the constant tiredness. On Sundays I often go to bed again straight after breakfast, in order to sleep.

Last Sunday I was sitting in the wood reading. Suddenly two men came from the bushes towards me. When they called to me I took flight, for I remembered all the rapes recently. I walked very fast and didn't stop even when they called. When I arrived in the village, one of them, not a German, came after me by bike. He said I was suspected of having stolen a bike. I fled into the house of Fräulein Schmidt, where I cried and was so upset. Silly! I felt very embarrassed afterwards.

8th July 1945

Yesterday I managed to give a letter to an unknown lady from Kempten, who is going to Hamburg soon. I hope it will arrive. It only has a short greeting and my address. I learned recently that passes in Kempten are still not being issued. So I have to keep on waiting. Yesterday I got a newspaper to read. Apparently Hitler was poisoned on April 27th. Rippentropp was arrested in Hamburg. Sundays are really miserable, because one has time to think. Nevertheless one looks forward to it for the whole week. I wonder why.

Sunday 15th July 1945

Again such a wretched Sunday. The other helpers have gone home and won't be back for a few days. The day before yesterday the little baby was born. The farmer's wife went home earlier from the field, and during lunch we heard her screaming terribly. It is a little baby boy.

22nd July 1945

On Sundays I usually sleep in the wood or read books. Today I had a row with the farmer's wife. She was cross that I had been away for two consecutive Sundays, instead of helping. But I don't see why. I work early mornings and evenings in the stable and I should be allowed to go to the woods for a few hours on Sunday. The other harvest helpers are lucky; they can escape to their homes. Jobs which I did voluntarily at first are now taken for granted. Perhaps it was premature of me when I said one and a half months ago that the farmers here show understanding.

Every fortnight a newspaper is published, but there is only rubbish about the Nazis in it. We still get bread, even some extra. Because of the shortages they have to harvest the new potatoes early. Along the road some are being stolen from the fields. I have got brown after all on my neck and arms. It has taken long enough. Unfortunately there is no opportunity to bathe except for the well in front of the house. At the moment, I am eating the first unripe apple. When they were in blossom I left Constance. Three months ago! I have to go to Kempten again in the next few days, to enquire about the transport for evacuees.

28th July 1945

Having cycled to Kempten every day since Tuesday (12km) and having queued there in vain for a pass (often six and a half hours in extreme heat or in rain) I have decided now to set off on Monday without a pass. That is to say, I shall simply stand on the Iller Bridge where, hopefully, a car will pick me up. I have managed to get an identity card and organised the cancellation of my police registration and the ration cards. I am very afraid of the second big trip, without papers, but it just has to be, because for four days I haven't had much work to do. After all my trips to Kempten the farmers don't want me any more and they want to get rid of me. I did not expect that from them. Like cattle, no milk, then away with it.

30th July 1945 – Beginning of the Long Journey

This is the second time I write this title. I hope it works out this time. This morning at 9 o'clock I started. I cried a little. I walked to Kempten. There, at 4 o'clock, I got a car up to 12km from Augsburg. I am staying overnight with a very nice lady. I only wish that I could make progress like this every day! I am still suffering from the weeping burns. There is a rash on my face and on my body, which itches and burns. I feel so silly and embarrassed on the journey. Today, before I left Kempten I witnessed a big car accident. A broken skull and both legs crushed. He will probably die.

I cannot see mountains any more. Thank Goodness! More and more wheat and less hay.

31st July 1945

I reached Augsburg by car. Here, too, there is devastation, but still life goes on quite busily. The accommodation is in a mass camp. Tomorrow morning at 6 o'clock I will go on. For the moment I have no difficulties in terms of food.

The rash on my body is getting worse. I can hardly sleep at night because of it. I suffer headaches and my face is red and swollen. I went to the hospital today for 3 Marks. There they gave me calcium injections. Afterwards I felt giddy.

1st August 1945

The rash is no worse, but about the same. I got up at 4.30 a.m. and went by car to Nürnberg (140km). There are ruins everywhere, but the food is quite good. Then I took a goods train using the pass of an unknown woman almost as far as Bamberg. I walked 2km with luggage, and then a car took me for 10km. Now I am in Bamberg. The food is worse and there are no cafés or inns. Tomorrow I will go on. Today I have been travelling from 5 o'clock in the morning until 8 o'clock in the evening and managed 200km which is quite an achievement. I am now totally worn out and tired. A nun gave me the address for accommodation with a private office lady. On the way from Augsburg to Nürnberg I saw fields of hop for the first time, of which Li told me already. Also fields of beet and clover are new. The meadows are totally different. Here near Bamberg there are fields of rape.

4th August 1945

On August 1st I went from Bamberg by car via Hassfurt to Schweinfurt. Many vineyards. I met travellers with the same destination: Hamburg. Schweinfurt is badly bombed and there is not much re-building going on. From there I took a goods train via Würzburg and Aschaffenburg to Hanau. The Bavarian ration cards, which I had, are now invalid. But I won't miss a train just because of some shopping in Bavaria. I couldn't know that the train would go that far. Anyway, soon I will get new ration cards in Hamburg. Up to then I will just have to go hungry. In Hanau the train stopped for four hours in the middle of nowhere. The night drew in and people made a camp fire and brewed some tea. At 12 midnight we continued, in an open goods train. It was bitterly cold. I slept very little. At 6 o'clock we reached Bebra and then caught a normal train up to Kassel, where controls were stricter. From here tickets were needed, but none were available for me. I went on foot with my heavy rucksack to the Reichsautobahn [Reichs motorway] and from there by car almost as far as Eichenberg. I smuggled myself through the barrier and went as a stow-away up to Göttingen. I didn't visit Buli there, because I couldn't get off the platform without a ticket. I went by goods train up to Kreiensen. For the second night I hardly slept and I was very cold. In the morning I caught an over-crowded train up to Bremen. As there was no connection I sat on some grass and waited.

Finally I got a ticket to Hamburg-Harburg without being questioned. In the evening I got as far as Harburg, but because of the curfew I had to spend yet another night on the platform. Exhausted, I slept on my blanket.

5th August 1945

I arrive home at 7 o'clock in the morning. Everyone in the family is fine. Inside the house so much has changed. There are now bombed out and homeless people finding shelter here. The street round about totally destroyed.

Utterly tired, utterly happy.

Hilke after the war, late 1945.

Postscript

Back in Hamburg Hilke completed her school education and then trained to become a nurse. Somehow, she hardly ever talked about the hard times immediately after the end of the war and her desperate efforts to get back home. I do not think that our parents ever read her diary, and we siblings certainly did not. Times were difficult in a different way. There was never enough food for the seven of us. Our father, being a lawyer, did not believe in black market business, and the slices of bread for each of us were carefully counted. I remember collecting fresh nettles to supplement our vegetables and we also went out to gather mushrooms and wild berries. Occasionally we even had to resort to eating beech nuts and roasted acorns, which tasted very bitter. It was a great help that we children were given school dinners. Each day we had thick hot soup provided by the British Red Cross, and before holidays we received a little parcel with food like tins of chicken soup and chocolate. Our house was also very cold. There was only one room kept warm by a stove for which we children collected wood.

However, on the whole we were happy because we were all back together and our parents taught us new values and a new sense of priorities in life. The university offered public lectures in

Hilke, Geseke, Brigitte and Regine in the early 1950s.

the evening and also in the churches some outstanding ministers preached about forgiveness and about Germany apologising for the wrong it had done.

Our father never really recovered from the strain of living through the war. For our mother it was very hard work, particularly as our father was no good at helping with practical things. Some months after the end of the war our father was badly injured when a bomb-damaged roof collapsed on top of him whilst he was having a hot soup in the railway station café.

Everything took a long time, for example cooking pea soup had to be done during the night as the gas pressure was not sufficient during the day. After two hours' cooking the hot saucepan with the soup was wrapped in newspapers and blankets to continue cooking until morning. Our mother used curtains to make dresses and the tips of shoes were cut off to make room for growing feet.

Our father with Hamburg's Bürgermeister Sieveking at a tennis tournament in the 1950s.

Our father in the 1950s organising the tennis tournament in Hamburg.

Hilke in her nurse's uniform.

Above: *Hilke in Heidelberg.*
Left: *Malcolm, c. 1956.*

In 1957 Hilke married Victor Malcolm Clark, a lecturer in organic chemistry at Cambridge University. They met in Heidelberg where Hilke was working as a nurse in the American hospital. She was introduced to Malcolm by John Hachenburg and his wife, a Jewish couple who had fled to England during the Hitler regime. After the war most Jewish refugees stayed in England, but the Hachenburgs, with a forgiving mind, went back to Germany where John became a judge in Heidelberg. He was always grateful to the English people for the hospitality he had been given during the war, and when Heidelberg University was looking for host families for the Cambridge Singers visiting Heidelberg to give a concert, he was eager to take a guest. This was Malcolm.

Left: *Hilke and Malcolm's wedding in Heidelberg, September 1957.*

Below: *Hilke and Malcolm in a decorated wedding car.*

Above: *Hilke with a birthday cake made by Malcolm.*

Right: *Hilke with her new baby boy, Duncan.*

After the wedding Hilke moved to Cambridge and in February 1959 she had a baby boy. A few happy months were given to the young family until, on 1 July, while travelling to the show *West Side Story* in London, they had a car accident. Hilke was killed instantly, the baby was unharmed in a carry cot, and Malcolm suffered a leg injury. It was a colossal blow to everyone involved, including Hilke's family in Hamburg. Our mother flew (for the first time in her life) to England to collect the baby and bring him home to Hamburg, whilst Malcolm recovered in hospital. When he was well enough to travel he joined the family in Hamburg where he watched his beloved son being cared for by Hilke's mother and Geseke. At the end of the summer Malcolm and the baby, who was christened Duncan, returned to England, but they came back for long Christmas and Easter holidays. During term time Duncan was looked after by his English grandmother.

At Hilke's funeral Malcolm gave a speech addressing her, in which he said:

Far left: *Hilke with Duncan, February 1959.*

Left: *Hilke in 1959.*

Below: *Hilke playing with baby Duncan, May 1959.*

Our edifice is broken and the largest piece has gone. In going the other pieces have changed and yet they stay together through you. With your help I must put them together again. I shall put them together again. A mighty door has been slammed, but perhaps, in this act, other doors have been opened.

At Easter 1960 Malcolm and Geseke became engaged. They were married in July, a year after the car accident. It felt natural and easy for Geseke to become Duncan's mother and, in time, she and Malcolm had three more children, Andrew, Gordon and Hilary.

Above: *Geseke and Brigitte wearing tops Geske had brought back from Italy, 1953.*

Right: *Geseke, 1954.*

Geseke and Malcolm at their wedding in Hamburg in 1960.

Geseke with baby Andrew in early 1962.

Right: *Geseke with the four children in front of the family's house in Warwick.*

Below left: *Geseke in Warwick, 1966.*

Below right: *Geseke in Hamburg, 1959.*

Background Notes

Birthdates of the five siblings:

Henning   January 1927
Hilke   April 1929
Geseke   February 1934
Brigitte   June 1937
Regine   October 1942

Henning's Story

In the autumn of 1944 Henning became a soldier in the German army. He was with the infantry. Before that – in fact, since spring 1943 – he was a so-called helper with the Air Defence, i.e. he was ordered away from the Hitler Youth, to which every boy and every girl was forced to belong, to join the Home Air Defence (*Flugabwehrbatterie* or FLAK). Each boy from his class at school from the age of sixteen, including Henning, joined one battery. They were accommodated in barracks and every day they wore old uniforms without decorations from soldiers of the

Air Defence. Otherwise, for visiting families in the city once a fortnight, for example, they wore the grey Hitler Youth uniforms of the Air Defence with the symbols of the Hitler Youth. When there was no alarm the teachers from the Johanneum School would come to the battery in the morning and give lessons (only main subjects). Officers, together with old soldiers, also came (the young ones were at the front) and taught military science and the handling of guns and air defence machines. When there was an alarm there was hardly any difference between the tasks of the old soldiers and those of the boys of the Hitler Youth.

Our brother Henning.

Geseke's Story

At the beginning of the war, in December 1939, when Geseke was five, she and two of her sisters were evacuated from Hamburg to stay with relatives in Meisenheim near Frankfurt. In July 1941 they returned to Hamburg for a few months.

From spring 1942 up until January 1945 Geseke lived with the wonderful von der Linde family in Dorow, East Pomerania, south of Kolberg, where she was meant to be a companion for the youngest daughter, Meike. However, it was not easy to get on with her, as Meike was one and a half years older and had very different interests. Geseke was often homesick.

In July 1943 she came home to Hamburg for the summer holidays, just when the heavy air raids, the 'firestorm', took place. The next day through radio announcements all mothers and children were asked to leave Hamburg immediately, as more air raids were expected. Our parents decided that Geseke, Brigitte and the sixteen-year-old au-pair, Clara, should go back to Dorow. As no station was functioning in Hamburg, they had to go by lorry as far as Langenhorn. There they found thousands of people who were also fleeing the city. They got on an overcrowded train, each with three little pieces of luggage, but they soon found out that this train did not go to Stettin (where they were meant to change trains) but to Schneidemühl, so they clambered out of the train, just in time. On the platform Clara and Brigitte started to cry and Geseke enquired from a railway official which train they should take. He put them on a military train. They were sitting on the laps of soldiers travelling to Stettin for two days and one night. Geseke remembers being given sweets by the soldiers.

On arrival in Dorow Geseke found that other children from Berlin had been welcomed by the family. They were of a similar age to Meike and Geseke, so it was decided to engage a private teacher who taught the five of them in the nursery. In January 1945 Geseke and Meike were taken by relations from East Prussia who were fleeing from the Russians. In two covered horse-drawn trucks they travelled west. With the Russians only 5km away they had to stop at the frozen river Oder near Stettin in order to let the two pairs of horses pull the first truck across the slippery ice, and then repeat the manoeuvre with the second truck. Finally, they arrived in Hamburg in the middle of February where Meike and, later, the rest of her family were given hospitality by Geseke's parents.*

---

* *In a telephone conversation in December 2007 Meike was pleased that she and her family were part of this account.*

Geseke and Brigitte, c.1953.

Brigitte's Story

Brigitte, only six years old after the Hamburg firestorm in 1943, was too young to stay in Dorow, so our parents decided to send her to a children's home in Thüringen, where she lived for over two years. It was a lonely time for her there, especially immediately after the war, when all the other children had been collected to come home. Brigitte was the only child remaining and the owner of the children's home lived in fear of the Russian occupation forces. For several months Brigitte's parents lost all contact with the home and with Brigitte. The Russians were fiercely guarding the borders between their zone and the British zone. Still, many people tried to escape from the Russian zone, particularly at night. Many were killed in search of freedom. Then, in the autumn of 1945, an eighty-year-old aunt and her sixty-year-old daughter picked up Brigitte and with the help of a guide, crossed the *grüne Grenze* (green border) by night. Wearing warm, dark clothes they had to be silent and crouch in ditches whenever the search light passed over the area. Later, on the open road, they heard the shots of Russian soldiers in the distance behind them. They arrived in Hamburg in November 1945 on an unforgettable day of joy and grateful relief.

Regine's Story

Regine, too young to be evacuated on her own, stayed with our mother throughout the war. In July 1943 our mother fled from the burning city of Hamburg with the nine-month-old baby in an open lorry. At one point when the little one kept crying the lorry driver allowed the baby to sit next to him in the front, so she could see better. This stopped her crying, but when the vehicle came to a brief halt a strange woman snatched the baby and jumped off the lorry with her. Luckily our mother noticed just in time and Regine was rescued.

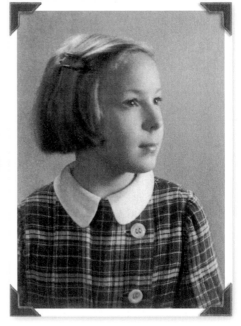

Above: *Regine, c.1950.*

Right: *Regine, c.1951.*

Deutsche Heimschule

The *Deutsche Heimschule, Oberschule für Mädchen* was accommodated in the Marianum, a private Catholic school belonging to the Hegne Monastery on Lake Constance.

In 1943 this school was taken over by the NSDAP (National-Socialist Workers' Party of Germany) in order to establish a school where young people would be indoctrinated with the new national-political ideas. The Sisters of the monastery had to leave and national-socialist teachers were installed. Due to the effects of the war (parents in cities were looking for boarding schools for their daughters away from the dangers of air raids) the numbers of girls grew to 357. This meant that some of the girls had to be temporarily accommodated in empty buildings of the Napola school for boys in Reichenau that had previously been used for housing mentally ill people.

On 17 April 1945 younger pupils were sent home. Some were sent to farms nearby and others had to work in the kitchen of the hospital in Constance. On 25 April the French army moved in and the headmistress was taken prisoner. In October 1949 the Marianum was returned to the Sisters. Now it is a flourishing secondary school offering different courses for career training.

Hilke's school on Lake Constance.

Pupils of the school peeling apples. Hilke is on the far right.

Hilke's school and pupils.

St Nikolai Church

The following is taken from an explanatory plaque erected on a viewing platform on the top of the spire of St Nikolai church, Hamburg. The church had been bombed in the air raid of July 1943 and only the spire is still standing today as a poignant reminder, much like the ruins of the old Coventry Cathedral.

Hamburg is one of the cities most affected by air raids during the Second World War. Most momentous among the aerial attacks on the city were the bombings that occurred between 25 July and 3 August 1943. The Royal Air Force, commanded by Air Marshal Arthur Harris (Bomber Harris), bombed Hamburg's residential areas for several nights in a row, aiming to demoralise the German population while the US attacked U-boat shipyards and armament factories during the day. Operation Gomorrha reduced large parts of the city to ashes; 35,000 people died in the flames, among them thousands of slave labourers who had been deported to Germany from other European countries, and over 5,000 children. Around one million inhabitants fled the city and the number of injured people is estimated at over 120,000.

Hamburg's eastern areas were especially hard hit. The three districts of Hammerbrook, Rothenburgsort and Hamm-Süd were completely destroyed by the firestorm and had to be declared prohibited areas. Prisoners from Neuengamme concentration camp were forced to recover the bodies, clear the rubble and defuse the bombs.

The images of destruction remind us of the cruelty which Nazi Germany spread all over Europe with its war of aggression and annihilation. It has been rightfully pointed out that the carpet bombings of residential areas were in breach of international law, cruel and not the right instrument for breaking the German masses' loyalty to Hitler. However, the fuse for the firestorm was lit in Germany. The German air raids on Guernica (1937), Warsaw (1939), Coventry and Rotterdam (1940), London (1941) and many other cities in Western and Eastern Europe preceded the destruction of Hamburg.

Courtesy of Dr Detlev Garbe

Timeline

1929

20 April　　　*Hilke is born in Hamburg, the second of five children.*

1939

1 September　Hitler invades Poland. Britain and France declare war on
　　　　　　　Germany two days later.

27 December　*Hilke is evacuated to Aunt Erica and Uncle Herbert in Meisenheim.*

1940

　　　　　　　The German Blitzkrieg overwhelms Belgium, Holland
　　　　　　　and France.

May　　　　　Churchill becomes Prime Minister of Britain.

May–June　　British Expeditionary Force evacuated from Dunkirk.

27 July　　　*Hilke starts her diary having been away from home for seven*
　　　　　　　months.

October　　　British victory in Battle of Britain forces Hitler to
　　　　　　　postpone invasion plans.

1941

　　　　　　　The Blitz continues against Britain's major cities.
　　　　　　　Mass murder of Jewish people at Auschwitz begins.

18 February	*Hilke arrives back home in Hamburg.*
June	Hitler begins Operation Barbarossa – the invasion of Russia.
October	General von Manstein's infantry has defeated the Romanian army of General Dumitrescu.
October	The German army breaks through the defence line by Odessa. Odessa is in flames.
November	Simferopol, the capital of the Crimea taken.
November	British air raids in Hamburg aimed at civilian homes.
December	Japan attacks Pearl Harbour and the US enters the war.

1942

	Germany suffers setbacks at Stalingrad and El Alamein.
9 April	*Hilke is told that her mother is expecting her fifth child at the end of September.*
26 July	*Big air raid on Hamburg; Hilke's home was spared though many houses nearby were destroyed.*
30 July	*Hilke is evacuated to an estate near Würzburg to be educated with the daughter there.*
Christmas holidays	*Baby Regine christened in a memorable family celebration.*

1943

February	Heroic battles at Stalingrad. The 6th Army is surrounded and their eventual surrender marks Germany's first major defeat.
	British and Indian forces fight Japanese forces.
24–25 July	Horrific air raids over Hamburg resulting in the terrible firestorm. All women and children have to leave the city.
September	Italy surrenders.

1944

January	*Hilke evacuated to the boarding school on Lake Constance.*
6 June	D-Day: The Allied invasion of France commences.
August	Paris liberated.
24 June	*Hilke's school celebrates the Summer Solstice.*
July	*A lovely summer family holiday in the Luneburger Heide.*
3 September	*Hilke's school suspended, only to be restarted in October.*

1945

27 January	Auschwitz liberated by Soviet troops.
12 March	*Commemorative service at Hilke's school for 'our' fallen heroes.*
18 April	*Hilke's school closes, leaving the pupils in the streets with just 30 Reichsmark each and no responsible adult to help them get home. There was no telephone and no postal service.*
20 April	*Hilke's sixteenth birthday. There is no letter from home, so she reads the letter she received for her previous birthday.*
25 April	*In the area around Hilke's school all pictures of Hitler are burnt and flags torn to bits.*
April	Russians reach Berlin.
30 April	Hitler commits suicide.
7 May	Germany surrenders.
8 May	The end of the war is declared – VE Day in Europe. Attlee replaces Churchill as Prime Minister of the UK and Truman becomes President of the US on Roosevelt's death.
26 May	*Beginning of Hilke's big journey home.*
5 August	*Hilke finally arrives home.*
6 August	Atomic bomb dropped on Japanese city of Hiroshima.
14 August	Japan surrenders in the wake of the atomic bombs on Hiroshima and Nagasaki.

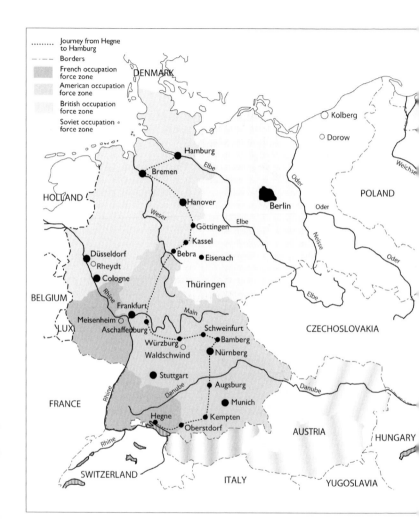

Maps

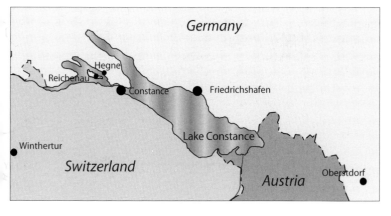

Above: *The area around Lake Constance.*
Opposite: *Hilke's route across Germany.*

If you are interested in purchasing other books published by Tempus,
or in case you have difficulty finding any Tempus books in your local bookshop,
you can also place orders directly through our website

www.thehistorypress.co.uk